How to Exercise Your Human

A cat's purrsonal training guide to a healthy homosapien

Robert W. Moore

SHOKO BOOKS

SHOKO
— BOOKS —

Published by ShoKo Books

www.ShortyandKodi.com
info@ShortyandKodi.com

ISBN-978-0-9921461-0-8

Disclaimer Claws

Before beginning this or any exercise program, we recommend taking your human to the vet to be poked and prodded by cold metal objects and even colder hands, all while being told *wut a good wittul kitteh cat they are!* And don't forget these two words: rectal thermometer.

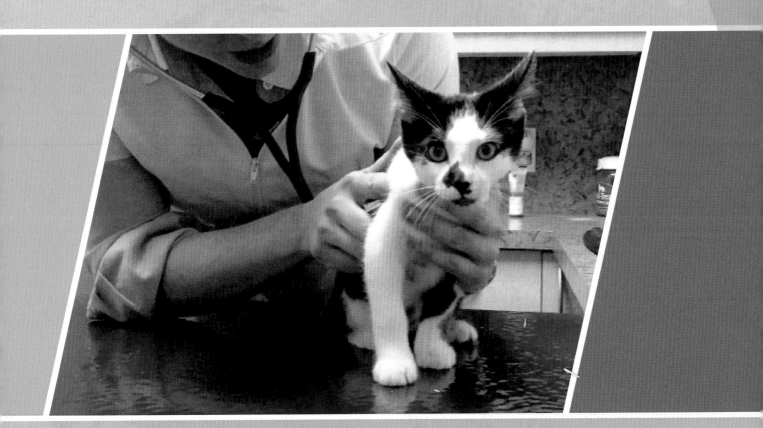

Introduction

Dear Fellow Felines,

Contrary to popular opinion, humans aren't entirely useless; like canines, they're large and messy but they do have opposable thumbs. And until we figure out how to open cans of tuna on our own, we're going to have to keep humans around a little longer.

Problem is, they're getting soft. We're hearing that obesity is an epidemic. Obesity is a medical condition in which humans can't carry home enough food for us. Its side effects are severe: a smaller bag of dry food in the cupboard, just a few cans of wet food in the fridge, and empty food dishes half-filled with food. Obesity is truly a nightmare.

So far, we have raised our human pets well. They pick up our poop, clean up our hairballs and allow their dogs to eat both while we lay in the sun. That's some good work, kittens. We know you don't want to hear this, but it's time to wake up!

Now that you're awake (you can nap later), let's talk about responsibility. If we're going to remain in the lifestyle to which we're accustomed, we have to take better care of our humans or else we'll be forced to return to the wild to fend for ourselves. You might think that's an option, but I have news for you: tuna don't grow in cans, kittens. They're out, like, in the middle of the ocean! And imagine a world with no clean, warm laundry to spread our fur on. No more computer keyboards to rest on while people are using them. No more nom-noms or treat-treats. And no more people pooper scoopers! Say it with us: people ... pooper ... scoopers.

So smooth out your whiskers and let's get to work to restore the balance of nature so we can get back to our 17th nap of the day knowing our food bowls runneth over. All you need are the tools in this book and a firm paw to make it happen. You might need your human as well to turn the pages; remember, that's their one saving grace: thumbs.

Sincerely,
Shorty and Kodi

> The Warm-Up

Humans need to warm up before exercise to reduce their chance of ~~complaining~~ injury. Since they are unreasonable creatures who do things like sleep at night and set objects upright on tables, exploit their desires to get them moving:

- at 4 a.m. meow at the top of your lungs and don't stop until they come running

- jump around and start knocking things down until they start picking them up

- wake up their computer by walking on the keyboard and keep pressing until you hear screaming

- Give them the toy wand they bought for you and hold on as you lead them around the house for a walk (see right)

Jumping is a great way for your human to warm up. It will also help them to catch birds mid-flight which would increase their usefulness. Show them how it's done and get the hairball out of there or they'll land on your tail and blame you for getting in the way. Clumsy humans.

PURRSONAL TRAINING TIP

Many people fail at exercise programs because they do too much too soon. Just a few exercises a day is fine at first! Don't bite off more than you can chew and take kitten steps while focusing on your goal of a ~~subservient~~ fit human.

Think outside the litterbox and try new things to get your human moving like stealing their clothes to make them chase you around. And if you really want to see them run, start clawing the furniture and rummaging through the plants. It's surprising how fast they can move with the right motivation!

PURRSONAL TRAINING TIP

Your human is warmed-up when they start to breathe heavy and purrspirate.
If they're panting while resting though, call the vet.

› The Workout

You've got your human off the couch, motivated, and warmed up. It's time to work out! For each exercise, we've listed 3 components to assist you in your training:

Purrpose: the way(s) in which your human will better serve you;

Mewvement: how your human should perform the exercise;

Cativity: what you can do to enhance each mewvement!

Remember, it's up to you if you want to fully participate, but since humans want to please us and crave positive reinforcement, it's best to have a paws-on approach to ~~scratch them~~ correct their technique. An obedient human is a happy human!

(1) Litterbox Squat

PURRPOSE: Bending down to clean the litterbox, pick up our food bowl, dispose of hairballs

MEWVEMENT: Human pushes hips back as if using the litterbox

CATIVITY: Lay limp in their arms for added weight or squirm around to give them a dynamic challenge

PURRSONAL TRAINING TIP

To keep a neutral spine, stick your butt out and lift your tail. Lift it higher. Now strut.

② Kitty Curl

PURRPOSE: Lifting bags of food, litter and us when we need a better vantage point for hunting

MEWVEMENT: Human bends the arm like they're feeding themselves; they've had a lot of practice

CATIVITY: Remain still, arched and ready to correct their technique

Humans are stubborn so making them work out may feel like a tug-of-war. But don't give up and, no matter how much they ~~bleed~~ beg, don't let go.

PURRSONAL TRAINING TIP

③ Furward Raise

PURRPOSE: Taking our food out of the cupboard, taking our litter to the trash, hanging cat pictures to honor us, holding us up to finally get that insect that's been on the wall for months

MEWVEMENT: Human raises arms forward

CATIVITY: Now's your chance! Catupult off your human's arm to get the bug on the wall! Oh, it's just a nail for the cat picture they never did hang up? Poop in their shoe.

PURRSONAL TRAINING TIP

Humans are creatures of habit and change can be scary. The best way to motivate them is to lead by example. Show them that no ~~fridge~~ ~~book shelf~~ ~~set of curtains~~ mountain is too high to climb!

④ Cateral Raise

PURRPOSE: Shoulder strength and stability to reduce turbulance in the cat carrier. Don't they know what we go through?

MEWVEMENT: Human raises arm to the side

CATIVITY: Lay limp and be thankful you're not in the cat carrier

PURRSONAL TRAINING TIP

Take full, deep breaths when exercising.

⑤ Lion King Press

PURRPOSE: Presenting us to the world. This is also useful because the human failed to provide an adequate descent route from the top of the climbing walls, or what they refer to as the "fridge", "book shelf", "curtains", etc., and we don't want them to drop us as they help us down. This exercise also prepares them for putting the book shelf back up, replacing the curtains and cleaning the top of the fridge — it's usually filthy up there!

MEWVEMENT: Human raises you over their head like the god you are

CATIVITY: Scout other climbing destinations

PURRSONAL TRAINING TIP

It's easy for humans to get distracted. For us cats, once we've got a goal in sight, we go for it! That's why our humans shouldn't get frustrated when they give us leather furniture, expensive drapes and other fragile things, because nothing will keep us from reaching for the ~~light fixture~~ stars. Keep your human focused by making small, clear goals that they can achieve, like cleaning up hairballs every morning, so they soon learn that nothing can stand in the way of ~~your~~ ~~their~~ your goals.

⑥ Puss-Up

PURRPOSE: Scrubbing our floor, fetching toys from under the couch, bowing before us

MEWVEMENT: Human gets close to the floor and finally sees it from our perspective and hopefully gets a mop

CATIVITY: Jump on their back and gently dig your claws in so they keep perfect form.

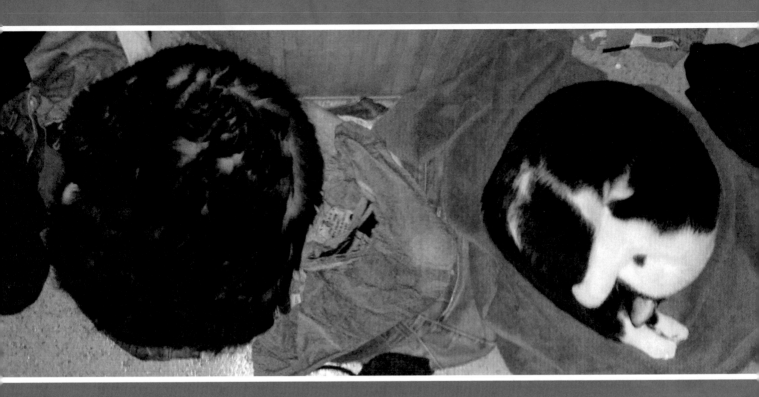

PURRSONAL
TRAINING
TIP

Household chores are a great way for your human to burn more calories. Find their dirty clothes and lie on them as a reminder to do the laundry. And lie on their clean clothes to get fur all over them so they have even more laundry to do! This will keep them active and they'll appreciate how thoughtful you are.

(7) Drop-me-and-you're Deadlift

PURRPOSE: It's not just a half-empty food bowl that makes us yowl through the night, it's a half-empty house! We need more food, more supplies, more more MEOW! If you want your human to bring home those big cat trees and extra-large kills, er, bags of food, it's time for advanced exercises like this.

MEWVEMENT: Human leans forward like they're cleaning our litterbox which they should really do a lot more often

CATIVITY: Lay comfortably in their arms to make yourself dead weight. If they drop you, poop in their shoes.

PURRSONAL TRAINING TIP

Did you know the sound of our purring actually decreases stress in humans and even boosts their immune system? For many of our stress-addicted humans, we are their only salvation when needing to relax. To maintain your regimen of 50 to 100 catnaps a day, your human must be relaxed. Under immense stress, your human will begin to bark, which is kind of like a dog's bark but with even more whining. You may lose your precious slumber to the barking of "bills", "kids", "holidays", or even "mother-in-law!" So, to protect your catnaps, jump on your human's lap and let your motor run. That way, you can get some rest while your human gets happy, healthy and very, very quiet.

⑧ The Catling Gun

PURRPOSE: 80% of humans will suffer a back injury which may cause a disruption in service. This exercise builds oblique and back strength so your human can continue uninterrupted service for the rest of their lives.

MEWVEMENT: Human leans to the side like they have a back-ache. They probably do.

CATIVITY: If you have a well-trained, obedient human, lean far back to go upside down to challenge their strength and so you can look really pretty.

PURRSONAL TRAINING TIP

To be a successful ~~dictator~~ Purrsonal Trainer, you have to take care of yourself first. We recommend a minimum of 18 hours a day of rest so you can be fully charged to train your human quickly and effectively. Plus, the more efficient you are, the sooner you can get back to sleep!

9 Cat Press

PURRPOSE: Pushing the heavy cart at the pet store that's filled with food, litter, treats, and a box of toys that we'll never play with because they're beneath us. Oh look, a box!

MEWVEMENT: Human on back showing their trust, presses arms up as if wanting a belly scratch

CATIVITY: Scratch their belly. See how they like it

PURRSONAL TRAINING TIP

Purrsonal training is hard work! We recommend a massage to loosen your joints and ease stress which will also keep your human's fingers strong for petting and working the can-opener.

⑩ Numbskullcrushers

PURRPOSE: To open our cans of food, humans need strong triceps, shoulders and chest muscles. And those thumbs.

MEWVEMENT: Human lies on their back and bends us over their head like, well, a numbskull

CATIVITY: Challenge your human's reflexes and work their muscles at the same time by swatting at their face occasionally and see how quickly they can shield themselves from your surprise attack.

PURRSONAL TRAINING TIP

Life is about balance (especially when walking along the curtain rod). Press pause on working so hard and allow your human to cuddle with you on the couch and watch some tv. They'll enjoy the bonding time which will increase their desire to serve you obediently and for eternity.

(11) Kitty Krunch

PURRPOSE: Strong abs helps our human get out of bed when we beckon for their service. Also, a strong human core is a better surface for us to pounce off if we are lying in their lap relaxing and they happen to sneeze or cough and we need to bolt for cover.

MEWVEMENT: Human on back lifts their torso up like they're going to lick their belly. They never do this but should learn if we're going to keep clean pets.

CATIVITY: Sit on their stomach to make sure they're holding their abs in. Dig your claws into excess belly fat as incentive, though they'll think it's a massage and say you're cute. Stupid humans.

Ecktherthithe ith fun! Don't take it too theriouthly.

⑫ Dog-in-the-Snow Plank

PURRPOSE: If humans are really going to be successful hunters, they have to learn to walk on all fours

MEWVEMENT: Human looks like a dog in the snow lifting their paws from the cold. Stupid dogs.

CATIVITY: Walk on their back and lift a paw and they'll copy us. Humans are happiest when they believe they are cats. Such simple creatures.

PURRSONAL TRAINING TIP

For your human to get stronger, they need more resistance.
Therefore, get bigger.
What they resist purrsists.

Humans, like cats, care a great deal about their appearance but they often feel bad about how they look. We don't know why; it's not their fault they've got no fur. Teach them to love the person staring back at them in the mirror and stop walking around as if they're wearing the cone of shame. Help your humans be proud of themselves, no matter what!

Having a workout buddy increases commitment!

› Stretching

Stretching is the best way to release tension but no matter how much we demonstrate it, humans haven't caught on. No wonder they're so stressed! Aside from grabbing them and helping them stretch, take every opportunity to lengthen out in front of them and show them how good it feels. A relaxed human is a happy human!

PURRSONAL TRAINING TIP

And since humans are embracing alternative therapy, apply catupuncture to anywhere your human needs it.

› Catgratulations!

You did it! By training your human you've taken a stand against an epurrdemic of laziness that threatens our own needs to be served, pampered, and to sleep 18 to 20 hours a day. You can rest, confident that your litter will be cleaned, your food bowl will be full and your happy human will be waiting with a warm lap and ready fingers to ensure your few waking hours are pleasant and stress-free.

Now here's the bad news. To keep your human in tip-top shape, you'll have to take them through this workout 2-3 times a week. After a few weeks, your human will be so proud and dedicated to serving you that they'll continue to do these exercises on their own!

Felines, because of us and our immense sacrifices, humans shall live on to serve us forever. For we, the humble domestic felines, the unsung heroes of humankind, have provided the answer to health and happiness that humans have sought for years: serve others, reach for our goals, take good care of us and love someone who makes you purr. Oh, and catnip. Lots of catnip.

Peace and purrs out,
Shorty & Kodi

Made in the USA
San Bernardino, CA
19 November 2015